STEAM into WESSEX

Right:
During the summer months photography at Waterloo was best in the late afternoon when the sun had moved into the west. Here is a pleasing picture of Salisbury-based rebuilt 'West Country' class Pacific, No 34013 *Okehampton*, which has just been given the road with the 5.43pm train to Salisbury. The driver has opened the cylinder cocks and the loco is easing forward under the signal gantry which displays 'MT', for the Main Through line out of Waterloo. Even towards the end of steam Salisbury engines were kept commendably clean and No 34013 was one of the best examples.

STEAM into
WESSEX

MIKE ESAU

IAN ALLAN LTD

First published 1991

ISBN 0 7110 1998 3

Published by Ian Allan Ltd, Shepperton, Surrey; and printed by Ian Allan Printing Ltd at their works at Coombelands in Runnymede, England

Front Cover:
'Steam into Wessex' — on a bright Sunday morning in the autumn of 1962, unrebuilt 'West Country' Pacific No 34002 *Salisbury* heads the down 'Bournemouth Belle' through New Malden station, the end of the 60mph speed limit out of London. There may have been a last minute failure at Nine Elms shed since *Salisbury* is not carrying the usual headboard and the normal motive power for this train was a rebuilt 'Merchant Navy'. No 34002 has the modified tender it acquired in April 1962 behind which is a British Railways built luggage van painted in Pullman colours to match the main train.

Previous page:
The exhaust from Standard Class 5 No 73029 merges with the clouds of a fine May evening as the locomotive pulls away from Wallers Ash loop south of Micheldever with an up train of 'Presflo' bulk cement wagons.

Below:
On a cold winter morning rebuilt Bulleid Pacific No 34037 *Clovelly* accelerates past the high down main line signal at Esher station with the 8.35am train from Waterloo to Weymouth.

Introduction

Since the original edition of this book was published over 20 years ago, a generation has grown up who did not experience the working steam era which finished on the Bournemouth and Weymouth line in the summer of 1967. This edition of *Steam into Wessex* will I hope bring to a new readership a portrait of the final 10 years of Britain's last main line passenger service regularly operated by steam power.

I am a regular traveller in and out of Waterloo and find it difficult to believe that so much time has passed since the station echoed to the sound of escaping steam and thunderous departures. The brief return of 'Merchant Navy' Pacific No 35028 *Clan Line* in October 1988 created the illusion that the locomotive's 'farewell to steam' working on 2 July 1967 had been but a year or two before; so enduring have been the images of that era. Now 23 years on, reminders of that time are being progressively swept away with the commencement of the momentous work at Waterloo on the construction of the International terminal.

My association with the line goes back to childhood since I was brought up in New Malden within earshot, if not sight, of the trains. Earliest memories are centred around the station or the nearby bridge which still affords such an excellent position from which to watch the frequent services. A highlight was the passage of a then brand new 'West Country' Pacific No 34099 *Lynmouth*, running light engine on the down local line, though it mysteriously turned off to take the Kingston route. Looking west from the bridge there was always an exciting sense of anticipation at the first hint of white steam appearing round the bend in the line at distant Surbiton, marked by the spire of St Mark's church. In the other direction, the approach of a down express through Raynes Park was often heralded by a pall of black smoke from the locomotive's fire being built up as the train accelerated out of the London area speed restrictions.

I first conceived the idea for *Steam into Wessex* in 1964 when laid up at home with 'flu, and decided to make a comprehensive portrait of the Waterloo to Weymouth route using the pictures I had already taken as a foundation. To bring a degree of organisation to the project I tasked myself with covering all the major stations and features along the line. I considered it essential to depict not only the locations and trains, but also the passengers and railway staff, subjects generally neglected by railway photog-

raphers. In between visits to other lines on the Southern or more distant parts of the country, I lost count of the journeys I made to places such as Basingstoke, Eastleigh and Weymouth, sometimes by train, or in my Austin 1100 car. In those days before the opening of the M3, improvements to roads such as the A30 and A31 and lower driving speeds, a round trip of some 270 miles from London to Weymouth meant far more hours behind the wheel than would be involved now.

From the time I took up railway photography in earnest in the mid-1950s, I have tried to diversify my approach to the subject. Whilst quite happy to use the classic three-quarter front view of trains when suited, there were many other times when a different treatment was essential, for example to emphasize weather conditions, special lighting or the character of a subject. The 1950s and 1960s was an exciting and inspiring period for railway photography, and without doubt the time when I took my most valued pictures. Sadly much contemporary steam railway photography seems to be centred around immaculately sharp 'set piece' three-quarter front views lit by full sun. I have to admit that a good deal of my work now has more in common with this approach than with the images from those heady days as steam neared its end, but then I suppose this a reflection of the inherently theatrical nature of steam operation today.

Looking back to the 1950s and 1960s, I am somewhat amazed that I had no thought or desire for wide angle or telephoto lenses, but the working steam railway was so rich in striking images that the standard lens seemed quite adequate with no need for different focal lengths to try to enhance a picture. I sometimes though travel back in time in my imagination and attempt to visualise the sort of pictures that would have been possible with a range of modern lenses and films.

Of course 20 or 30 years ago the choice of photographic equipment was comparatively limited — Japanese camera technology was only beginning to make its mark, and aids such as through the lens metering and zoom lenses which we take for granted today, were the exception rather than the rule. Throughout my railway photographic career I have always used medium format cameras for the majority of my work, and comment on this in the captions to some of the pictures. Apart from the higher quality of enlargement which is generally available from a larger negative or transparency, it is quite possible to use only part of the image area with little detrimental effect to the end result. 35mm does have its place because of its versatility, lenses with a good depth of field, and speed of operation which helps the alert photographer to capture spontaneous pictures. My main equipment today is the 6cm x 6cm Mamiya C330S camera with a range of lenses, an excellent and affordable system in a format which allows for cropping both vertically or horizontally if desired.

Whatever the equipment or treatment of the subject, my cardinal rule was, and still is, that the picture must be harmonious and pleasing to the eye, and I have tried to ensure that this applies to every image in *Steam into Wessex*.

Because of constraints on space, I had to omit some interesting material from the first edition, but have now taken the opportunity to replace some of the original pictures with new ones from the period, the majority of which I have printed for the first time. Thanks to the enduring nature of black and white prints, I have been able to re-use most of those I made for the book in the late 1960s. At that time I usually used Kodak Glossy Bromide paper developed in D163 which gave rich blacks and a wide range of tones. Where new prints have been required, it has proved quite difficult to match the brilliancy of my 1960s work with resin coated paper, but I hope the difference is not detectable. Modern paper does dry flat though and the smooth finish on the glossy paper is attractive to sight and touch. Its desirable qualities have saved the unproductive time I used to spend in the darkroom feeding crinkled prints on to a hot glazer, my eyes smarting from the effects of the pungent glazing solution.

The captions to the pictures in the original edition of the book were very brief, but these have now been considerably expanded. I am afraid I was very lax about keeping details of my pictures in steam days since most time and effort was expended on securing new material. Consequently the majority are undated though I hope this will not detract from their enjoyment and interest.

What of colour? In fact I took very little until the preservation era — for one thing the film was expensive compared to black and white material, and apart from this the emulsions were rather slow so that pictures needed good light to be successful. The passage of time too has shown that some colour emulsions have not proved to be stable, with effects ranging from total loss of the image to unacceptable colour changes. Moreover, some of the most evocative scenes in the working steam era were characterized by poor light or dirty engines, for which colour material would have been totally unsuited. Colour film was right though for the weather and the train on the dust jacket picture. Kodak Ektachrome 64 film was used in a 6cm x 6cm format Zeiss Super Ikonta camera fitted with an Opton Tessar lens and Synchro-Compur shutter.

It was in just such weather that I enjoyed a nostalgic train journey to Weymouth recently.

The third-rail electrification snaking down to distant Weymouth has made less visual impact on the line than the advent of 'Network South-East', with its cheerful red, white, blue and grey house colours, far removed from the predominantly muted green and maroon shades of steam days. Travel in one of the long open saloons of a Class 442 Network Express unit has a detached quality more in common with a flight in a Boeing 737 aircraft than a train, progress so rapid that familiar landmarks are passed unseen given a momentary lapse of concentration. All a sharp contrast to what seems now to be the leisurely schedule of the steam hauled express, the passenger installed on the deep upholstery in a Bulleid coach and lulled by the rhythm of the rail joints. Perhaps journeys after dark were best, such as one I made up from Eastleigh one cold clear winter night in an ex-works Maunsell saloon coach, its dynamo humming quietly as the train slowly increased speed on the climb toward Litchfield. The newly varnished woodwork creaked in the warm gently swaying coach, whilst outside the steamy windows, exhaust from the train's 'Lord Nelson' billowed white across the moonlit rolling contours of the Hampshire chalklands.

The chalklands are unchanged though many of the photographic locations would be unusable now due to the growth of lineside foliage. Towns along the route too have grown, notably Basingstoke whose office blocks and towers are soon reached after a brief interlude of meadowland which suddenly appears after woods of pine and silver birch sheltering red brick villas sunk among the trees. The passenger liners of steam days at Southampton have long vanished, but their modern cruise counterparts can be seen in the New Docks next to more mundane container ships moored alongside huge compounds full of newly imported cars.

Bournemouth retains its distinctive high roof, though the station is strangely quiet after the exuberant and noisy days of steam when each departure was something of a spectacle. Memories of this earlier age can come from unexpected quarters for my arrival coincided with the departure of the up 'Wessex Scot' to Glasgow Central, a smart rake of InterCity coaches hauled by a matching newly painted Class 47 diesel. Evocative names such as Crewe, Preston, Lancaster Oxenholme, Penrith echoed round the station, a reminder of the distant destinations of Somerset & Dorset line trains from Bournemouth West which slowly made their way north over the Mendips in summers past.

So on to busy Poole, crowds of shoppers waiting at the level crossing gates as the train curves into the station. At Wareham the trackless bay platform on the up side of the station is a reminder of hopes for the future now that the Swanage Railway has reached Corfe Castle. Then into the Dorset countryside past the River Frome, winding through bright green meadows set against the beckoning Purbeck Hills outlined grey against the horizon. After the line turns south at Dorchester, the climb through the downland gives no hint of the panorama of Weymouth and Portland awaiting as the train emerges from Bincombe tunnel and sweeps down to the sea. This short last stretch is perhaps still the most scenic part of the route, though much changed at Upwey and on the site of the shed at Weymouth, by the construction of large housing estates.

More especially on this western part of the route, or anywhere else in the country for that matter, it was quite unusual to come across other photographers out on the line in steam days. However, it was by the line at Wimbledon that I met my friend of more years standing than we both care to remember, Gerry Siviour (my co-author for *Waterloo-Exeter Heyday* [Ian Allan 1990]). Gerry has been of great assistance in checking the captions for the pictures and suggesting improvements, and I am indebted to him for this.

Similarly there was little opportunity to get to know footplate staff but by happy chance I met Peter Miller, then a driver at Weymouth shed, whose house I stayed at for bed and breakfast during one of my many visits to the area. Peter was very co-operative and some pictures of him appear in the book. He is now enjoying retirement in Weymouth and I recently spent a very pleasant afternoon with him and his wife Gwen, reliving the days of steam. I am most grateful to him for his help. I have also been fortunate enough in recent years to meet 'Bert Hooker, once a top link driver at Nine Elms, and a fireman during the 1948 Locomotive Interchange Trials. 'Bert is as enthusiastic as ever about locomotives, and has the wonderful ability to captivate individuals and audiences with his recollections of steam days on the Southern. He very kindly went through the pictures for the book with me and I have built into the captions his observations and comments made from the point of view of a 'professional'. My sincere thanks are due to him.

Mike Esau
November 1990

Below:
Bulleid Pacific nameplates — No 35007 *Aberdeen Commonwealth,* **No 35013** *Blue Funnel,* **No 35026** *Lamport & Holt Line,* **No 34015** *Exmouth,* **No 34056** *Croydon,* **and the shield of No 34006** *Bude.*

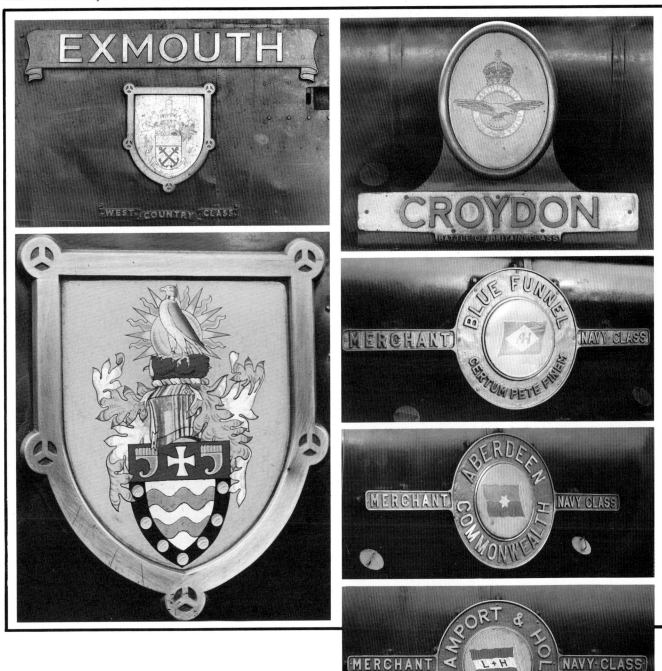

Above:
I took this picture at Waterloo on a fine summer evening showing part of the valve gear of a rebuilt Bulleid Pacific just as the driver eased the regulator open. The hissing steam gives some hint of the massive forces at work inside the cylinder.

Right:
The start from Waterloo could be a tricky one with a heavy train on a damp day because of the curvature of the platforms and the ban on the use of sanding equipment within the station limits to avoid affecting the track circuits. Here rebuilt 'Merchant Navy' Pacific No 35026 *Lamport & Holt Line* slips badly whilst starting the 1.30pm train to Bournemouth.

Left:
Four and a half miles out from Waterloo at Clapham Junction was a 40mph speed limit round the curve through the station, a typical running time from the terminus with an express train being 7 to 8 minutes. A Standard Class 5 4-6-0 is easing through the station before opening up again towards Earlsfield and Wimbledon. There are two distinct batches of coal on the tender. Newer, larger lumps, are at the front while sometimes the coal at the back remained untouched for lengthy periods of time. Note the TV rental advertisement on the Granada cinema on St John's Hill which proclaims 'Instant' TV on three channels.

Below:
Vauxhall station has changed little over the years apart from general smartening up in Network SouthEast colours. In the early 1960s Basingstoke remained a quiet provincial town with a modest service centred round stopping trains leaving Waterloo at 54 minutes past the hour. Motive power tended to be 'hand-me-downs' withdrawn from more onerous duties, and 'Schools' 4-4-0 No 30902 *Wellington* rumbling gently through Vauxhall station on the 1.54pm train is typical. In its heyday No 30902 was a St Leonards engine working on the Hastings line, but moved to the Western Section on the electrification of the South Eastern main lines.

Above:
An attractive platform canopy and oil lamps set off this picture of rebuilt 'West Country' Pacific No 34026 *Yes Tor* coming through Beaulieu Road station with an up train from Bournemouth and Weymouth to Waterloo. No 34026 was withdrawn in September 1966. The weather this spring day was that beloved by railway photographers, with heavy showers followed by brilliant clear light. Note the evidence of forthcoming electrification with the third-rail insulators in place on the down line and a further collection on the platform.

Left:
The rather more functional and austere canopies at Waterloo feature in this winter picture of two '82000' series 2-6-2Ts on empty stock duties watched by a small group of enthusiasts. The 2-6-2Ts provided overdue modern motive power for the haulage of heavy empty stock trains to Clapham Junction, but for the photographer the 'M7' 0-4-4Ts they replaced were greatly missed.

Above:
A disadvantage for the photographer was that much of the Waterloo to Weymouth line ran in an east to west direction and this made lighting conditions difficult after about mid-day especially for up trains in the summer. However, the canopy at Winchfield station acts not only as an effective lens hood for the camera, but also gives depth to this picture of rebuilt 'Merchant Navy' No 35012 *United States Lines* heading the up 'Bournemouth Belle'.

Left:
The west end of Woking station on a cold winter morning with a stiff breeze blowing from the north. A rebuilt Bulleid Pacific waits to leave with a down stopping train whilst a sister engine on an up Bournemouth service passes a Standard Class 4 4-6-0.

Above:
The line south of Micheldever ran along a small embankment in open country, which in the evening offered the chance of photographing up trains silhouetted against the sky. Here a rebuilt Bulleid Pacific climbs north up the 1 in 252 gradient one stormy evening just as the sun breaks through the scudding clouds.

Below:
Drifting smoke and steam from the soft exhaust of Bulleid Pacifics could prove troublesome for both enginemen and photographers especially when the loco was beginning its journey from 'cold'. In this early morning picture of No 34089 leaving Weymouth, the clean white steam forms an attractive pattern along the side of the train. No 34089 was distinguished by being the last steam locomotive to be repaired at Eastleigh works emerging from the shops on 3 October 1966.

Above right:
The lighting from the Reading line platforms at Clapham Junction as the sun moved round into the west could be very attractive for early evening trains. A rebuilt 'West Country' Pacific rounds the main line curve through the station on a down train, whilst in the carriage sidings two Standard Class 4 2-6-4Ts wait to leave for Waterloo with empty stock.

Below right:
The day has started brightly but clouds are building up at Woking as rebuilt 'Merchant Navy' No 35013 *Blue Funnel* speeds through the station with the 8.10am boat train from Waterloo to Weymouth. Unusually for this time of day the engine's headcode electric lights are on. At the adjacent up main line platform a Crompton Type 3 diesel waits to leave for Waterloo, while a London Country 'RT' bus on a local service can just be glimpsed to the left of the 'Merchant Navy'.

Above:
The LSWR pneumatic signals
were long a feature of the line
from Woking to Basingstoke
and this fine gantry guarded
the approach to Basingstoke
from the east, until
replacement by colour lights in
October 1966. Worth a picture
in their own right I waited
until dusk on a clear evening
and photographed the signals
silhouetted against the sky to
show off the lattice work and
arms to the best advantage.
The signals for the down slow
and fast through lines are 'off'.

Right:
A signalman's view from the
interior of Shawford Junction
box in 1962, as rebuilt 'Battle
of Britain' No 34053 *Sir Keith
Park* passes with an up train
from Bournemouth composed
of Bulleid and Standard
coaches. The Didcot, Newbury
& Southampton line, which
branches off to the left of the
picture, closed completely on
10 August 1964.

14

Left:
The approach to Southampton Central station is a tortuous one and was hemmed in by terraced houses in steam days. I stood in the garden of one of them to photograph Standard Class 5 No 73080 *Merlin* accelerating a down train from the 15mph speed check on the sharp curve at Northam and past the attractive Tunnel Junction signalbox. The box controlled the junction of the main line with the spur from Southampton Terminus which is seen coming in from the right.

Below:
The signalman's bicycle (though a ladies model!) is propped up outside West Byfleet signalbox as unrebuilt 'Battle of Britain' No 34057 *Biggin Hill* approaches the station with an up train. Note the lower than usual position of the down main line signal for sighting purposes and the white diamond on the lattice post indicating that the signal was track circuited. No 34057 survived until May 1967 to become one of the last unrebuilt Bulleid Pacifics in traffic.

In 1966 I was fortunate enough to win a Bronica S 6cm x 6cm single lens reflex camera in a photographic competition and this opened up new picture taking possibilities, where for example precise framing was required. The standard lens was a splendid 80mm f2.8 Nikkor with a very accurate focal plane shutter capable of stopping the fastest train, but sadly in the long term the camera proved to be temperamental and unreliable. These three pictures were taken with the Bronica and show *(left)* an up Channel Islands boat train hauled by a rebuilt Bulleid Pacific framed in a disused ganger's hut near Moreton and *(below)* a Standard Class 4 4-6-0 arriving at Parkstone station with an up train from Weymouth. This is seen through an attractive triangular cut out on the parapet of the concrete bridge which spanned the line. The third picture *(right)* called for very precise timing and depicts an up train hauled by rebuilt 'Merchant Navy' Pacific No 35030 *Elder-Dempster Lines*, framed in the '5' of a disused 15mph speed restriction sign. This sign marked the point where the then lifted branch from Abbotsbury joined the main line at Upwey & Broadwey station. The small overbridge in the background was the spot where drivers of fast down trains would start braking for arrival at Weymouth.

Above:

One of the benefits of taking pictures on the line between Winchester and Southampton was the additional trains from the Alton, Romsey, DNS and Fareham lines, worked by vintage motive power up to the late 1950s. Here Eastleigh shed's push and pull fitted 'M7' class 0-4-4T No 30029 pauses at Winchester with a train from Alton to Eastleigh. Often after a visit to Eastleigh I would come home via Alton in a LSWR push and pull set with an 'M7', and invariably an exhilarating descent from Medstead & Four Marks to Alton would produce speeds seemingly not far removed from the main line east of Basingstoke!

Right:

On a hot summer day in 1958 'T9' class 4-4-0 No 30313 waits to leave Eastleigh with a DNS line train for the 33-mile run to Newbury, across a land of rolling chalk downland and soaring skylarks. At this time 'T9s' and Collett 0-6-0s were typical motive power for this line. No 30313 was later transferred to Exmouth Junction shed to become one of the last 'T9s' in service, finishing its days on the North Cornwall line until withdrawal in July 1961.

Top:
A reminder that several of the main line trains between Southampton and Basingstoke were for destinations other than London. Here 'Lord Nelson' class 4-6-0 No 30860 *Lord Hawke* trundles northwards through St Denys station on the outskirts of Southampton with a through train for Newcastle composed of British Railways Standard Mk 1 stock, the first two coaches being in chocolate and cream livery. The locomotive is beginning the long climb to Litchfield tunnel and is probably being worked on the first regulator and about 20% cut-off. *Lord Hawke* would work through to Oxford before being replaced by a Western Region engine.

Above:
Classic Drummond designs at Eastleigh station in 1958. 'T9' 4-4-0 No 30313 has just arrived in the up local platform from the shed ready to work a train on the DNS line, whilst in the foreground, 'M7' class 0-4-4T No 30028 leaves with a two-coach train for the Fareham line composed most unusually of ex-LMS main line stock.

Above:
There was a fine gantry at St Denys controlling the Portsmouth and main lines. Eastleigh shed's 'T9' 4-4-0 No 30310 is curving gracefully beneath the gantry, with steam shut off, ready to stop at the station with a local train from Salisbury to Portsmouth. The stock is a three-coach Bulleid set with a Maunsell corridor bringing up the rear.

Right:
Basingstoke station was a rewarding place for photography particularly on summer Saturdays. Holiday extra trains brought many Western Region engines down the line from Reading, especially from the summer of 1963 with the re-routing of services which previously had used the Somerset & Dorset route. A wet day sees 'Hall' class 4-6-0 No 6924 *Grantley Hall* (though sadly bereft of nameplates) slipping in uncharacteristic fashion as it leaves Basingstoke with a train for Oxford and the north.

20

Above:
The Friday evening rush hour at Waterloo saw two departures to Bournemouth West at close intervals. On the right unrebuilt 'West Country' No 34038 *Lynton* is about to leave with the 5.23pm FO train whilst to the left rebuilt 'West Country' No 34018 *Axminster* is in charge of the 5.30pm. Both engines are carrying '70D' Eastleigh shed plates, the more familiar '71A' having disappeared following a change in the codes which became effective from 30 September 1963. Since dusk is approaching both engines have their electric light route indicators in use, though one of the lights on No 34018 appears not to be working so a trusty oil lamp is in place.

Left:
With the withdrawal of 'King Arthur' class No 30770 *Sir Prianius* in November 1962 the reign of this sturdy class came to an end. The last survivors spent most of their time working semi-fast services to and from Waterloo. Here is No 30798 *Sir Hectimere* after arrival at the terminus on a winter morning with a train from Salisbury where it was shedded. No 30798 was withdrawn in June 1962.

21

Right:
'The watchers' — the Bronica camera I mentioned earlier was excellent for more creative work, its large bright focusing screen making composition that much easier. Here at Waterloo on a dismal winter day and I have used the dark forms of these two enthusiasts to frame a train about to leave hauled by a rebuilt Bulleid Pacific. The f2.8 lens was more than adequate for these conditions provided the camera was loaded with HP3 film, which I usually developed in 'Promicrol' or 'Microphen'.

Below:
At Clapham Junction my then young brother-in-law Ian, peers intently at rebuilt Bulleid Pacific No 35030 *Elder-Dempster Lines* coasting through with the down 11.00am 'Atlantic Coast Express'. In 1962 the schedule allowed 80 minutes non-stop to Salisbury compared with a typical time of 83 minutes today with four stops using a Class 50 diesel. This platform at Clapham Junction remains a favoured position for spotters since it gives a good view of the Windsor, Main and Brighton lines.

Left:
The fireman of 'Merchant Navy' Pacific No 35026 *Lamport & Holt Line* contemplates the road ahead as the engine eases out of Waterloo with a train for Bournemouth. During the run the engine would typically use three to three and a half tons of Grade 2 Welsh Bedwas Colliery coal and about 5,000 gallons of water.

Below:
Mr Jarman, the motive power supervisor at Waterloo, passes on some instructions to the crew of rebuilt Bulleid Pacific No 34077 *603 Squadron*. The supervisor was located in a hut at the end of platform 11 from where he had a direct telephone line to the running foreman at Nine Elms shed.

Left:

As already noted sanding was prohibited in the environs of Waterloo station and here the driver of rebuilt Pacific No 34089 *602 Squadron* is having a job to control the engine on the greasy rails as it starts a train for Bournemouth.

Below

The Urie series of 'King Arthur' 4-6-0s were the first of the class to be withdrawn, Basingstoke shed's No 30748 *Vivien* going in September 1957. Here is the engine at Waterloo one hot summer afternoon waiting to work a semi-fast train to Basingstoke watched by a small group of spotters taking it easy on a luggage trolley. The engine is fitted with electric lights, but the conduit for the cables over the front buffer beam could be a hazard for footplate crews at night. To the right of the picture can be seen the large Type BR 1F tender (5,625gal water and 7ton coal capacity) fitted to the Southern's allocation of Standard Class 5 4-6-0s which replaced the 'King Arthur' class on their main line duties.

This page:

The high block of flats which still stands outside Waterloo is an excellent vantage point from which to photograph the trains. These two pictures were taken on a hot summer afternoon in 1958 and show *(above)* Feltham shed's Urie S15 No 30501 pressed into passenger service on the 3.54pm Waterloo to Basingstoke service composed of Maunsell coaches. Among the trains in the station, a rebuilt Bulleid Pacific is waiting departure, whilst to the far left another is just arriving. Unlike today St Paul's Cathedral still dominates the skyline, though the first of the City's tower blocks can be seen under construction. Turning in the other direction, *(below)* 'King Arthur' class 4-6-0 No 30783 *Sir Gillemere* is running across the arches on the approach to the station with a short boat train from Southampton Docks composed of Maunsell and Bulleid coaches, together with a Pullman car. A rake of 4COR electric units is passing bound for Portsmouth Harbour, whilst a Maunsell 4SUB rests in the sidings beyond.

This page:
Waterloo arrivals — *(right)* 'I know I had that case at Southampton' perhaps the pensive lady in the centre of the picture is thinking. A boat train has just arrived in the early afternoon and things are taking a bit of sorting out. Note the chauffeurs, the young lady in the 1960s style hat by the front of the engine and the BOAC advertisement. Rather earlier on a summer morning *(below)* in 1965 a commuter train originating at Salisbury has arrived at Platform 14 and the passengers are hurrying for the tube or bus. I have used a slow shutter speed to give a sense of movement to the picture. Three passengers are wearing bowler hats, headgear becoming increasingly rare nowadays. The poster on the far left is a reminder of the 'Classic' cinema which was located by Platform 1. It is showing the 1964 Paramount film 'The Carpetbaggers' starring George Peppard, Carroll Baker and Alan Ladd (his last film).

Facing page, top:
Most photographs at Bournemouth Central station seem to have been taken from the road bridge at the London end, but the interior of the station with its lofty roof could produce some attractive effects on a sunny day. Here an Ivatt 2-6-2T No 41224, one of a batch drafted in to replace the ageing 'M7' class tanks, is about to pull the Weymouth portion out of the platform ready for attachment to the rear of the main train from Bournemouth West which is due in a few minutes. This was one of the few places on British Railways where a shunting movement was permitted with loaded passenger coaches.

Facing page, bottom:
Another feature of Bournemouth Central was its long down platform which could take two separately signalled trains, and the western end was a favourite venue for spotters since it gave an excellent view of the shed opposite. Two devotees are studying the timetable for which a luggage trolley forms a convenient support. Of the graffiti, who was 'Stokes' I wonder and what was a 'No 6'?!

Most of the spotters in these pictures will be well into their 30s now, perhaps with children of their own, and I wonder how many are still interested in railways, or if any readers will recognize themselves. This charming study *(left)* was captured at Waterloo of what I think were a brother and sister taking down the details of a Standard Class 5 4-6-0. On another platform *(below left)* a group of more serious spotters have seized the chance to clean up the cab side of unrebuilt 'West Country' No 34038 *Lynton* before it backed out of the station to run to Nine Elms shed. At Bournemouth Central station *(below)* sister engine No 34102 *Lapford* is watched by two spotters as it pulls out of the station with empty stock, while to the left is one of the new blue liveried 4TC electric units. No 34102 was one of the last unrebuilt Bulleid Pacifics in service not being withdrawn until the end of steam in July 1967. Further down the same platform at Bournemouth *(right)* the graffiti shows that some loyalties lie outside the Southern and the creditable drawing of the 'A4' may have been inspired by the visit of No 60024 *Kingfisher* on a railtour to Weymouth in March 1966.

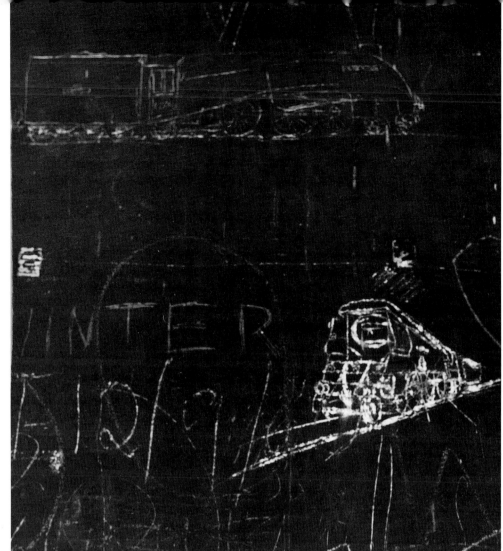

This page:
The 'Bournemouth Belle' 1931
to 1967 — The 'Bournemouth
Belle' brought a touch of
elegance to the workaday
routine on the line, and
happily survived to the end of
steam on the Southern. Under
the stylish board announcing
the train, *(left)* a smartly
dressed lady wearing a
memorable hat has her ticket
checked at the entrance to
Platform 11 before boarding.
An Ivatt 2-6-2T has brought in
the empty stock from Clapham
Junction yard and blows off
impatiently awaiting the
12.30pm departure time. At
the other end of the line at
Bournemouth Central *(below
left)* passengers wait to board
coaches 'H' and 'J', assisted by
smartly uniformed Pullman
staff.

Above right:
In its last years the up train
left Bournemouth Central at
4.37pm for the
2 hours 16 minutes run to
Waterloo with one stop at
Southampton Central.
Preceding it at 4.28pm was a
local train to Eastleigh which
the 'Belle' overtook on the
short four track section
through Pokesdown station.
Here Standard Class 5 4-6-0
No 73065 is on the local train
being passed by rebuilt 'West
Country' Pacific No 34044
hauling 10 cars and a luggage
van substituted for a Pullman
brake. It had been hoped that
the last 'Bournemouth Belle'
on 9 July 1967 would be steam-
hauled and worked by the then
senior driver at Nine Elms,
George Holloway. Sadly
though it was not to be and a
Class 47 diesel was used
instead.

Right:
In this 1962 picture an
immaculate rake of nine
Pullman cars is being
accelerated through Millbrook
station on the outskirts of
Southampton early on a crisp
autumn afternoon hauled by
rebuilt Bulleid Pacific
No 35024 *East Asiatic
Company.* The train was due
off Southampton Central
station at 2.01pm for its
39 minute run to
Bournemouth Central.

This page:
Low winter light (*above*) shows off the pleasing design of No 35014 *Nederland Line* as it comes through Vauxhall station with the down train, whilst further west (*left*) in a smoky cutting near Hook the down 'Belle' passes an up train.

Opposite:
I had spent much of a golden October day with my camera on the Basingstoke to Winchester section and finished up at Roundwood signalbox to await the up 'Bournemouth Belle'. Though the box had closed for the winter it was alive with the buzz of a myriad of insects which danced behind its dusty windows. By half past five I had moved a few hundred yards down the line to where the weakening rays of the sun cast long russet shadows across the ploughed field to my right as a damp chill came to the still air. The train was due off Southampton Central at 5.15pm and would be through Roundwood in about 25 minutes. It was late — would the sun last? But then a deep rumble as the 'Belle' left Popham tunnels before the first majestic sight of rebuilt 'Merchant Navy' No 35003 *Royal Mail* working hard up the 1 in 252 gradient.

Above:
Sunday engineering work would invariably produce some interesting pictures such as these taken in the summer of 1959 from the small bridge on the east side of New Malden station. Track re-laying is being carried out on the down lines while 'U' class 2-6-0 No 31612 *(above left)* is passing by cautiously on the up slow with an empty stock train routed via East Putney consisting of a Southern Railway bogie luggage van and a Maunsell 3rd corridor coach. Meanwhile in the opposite direction *(above right)* the down 'Bournemouth Belle' hauled by rebuilt Bulleid Pacific No 35020 *Bibby Line* is approaching the station on what is normally the up fast line. *Bibby Line* was reputed to be among the best of the rebuilt 'Merchant Navy' class. The train will probably have crossed over for wrong line working on the Waterloo side of Raynes Park.

Left:
Early on an autumn morning rebuilt Bulleid Pacific No 35026 *Lamport & Holt Line* climbs away up the long straight from Winchester with an up train for Waterloo. The line was closely bordered by trees along this stretch and falling leaves could make the rails very slippery in the autumn especially in damp cuttings.

In its 143 miles the Waterloo to Weymouth line passed through only six tunnels and of these five were between Basingstoke and Southampton. In the first picture *(above)* a Standard Class 5 4-6-0 is about to enter the dank interior of the very wet Southampton tunnel. The view is from the front coach of a steam-hauled down train and the fireman is leaning from the cab as the engine approaches the exit. When travelling on the train I was always on the look-out for unusual pictures and in this one *(left)* have managed to capture another Standard Class 5 No 73089 *Maid of Astolat* bursting out from the north end of Wallers Ash tunnel. In the third picture *(right)* rebuilt Bulleid Pacific No 34017 *Ilfracombe* is at the closely spaced Popham No 1 and No 2 tunnels with a down train.

Left:
This high position at Bincombe tunnel affords a good view of the tender of rebuilt 'Merchant Navy' No 35023 *Holland-Afrika Line* which sadly by this time did not carry its nameplates. The driver will have the blower on and is sounding the engine's whistle as it plunges into the darkness on the descent to Weymouth, and to keep the dust down the fireman has operated the coal washers on the tender. Bincombe was a dry tunnel though it could become uncomfortably full of smoke and steam especially if the wind was blowing off the sea against the southern portal pushing the fumes back into the bore.

Below left:
The morning sun shows up rebuilt 'West Country' No 34018 *Axminster* as it emerges from Popham No 1 tunnel with an up train. The down distant signal for Micheldever is on the left of the picture.

This page:
The line from Dorchester to Weymouth was finely aligned as this picture *(above)* shows. No 35003 *Royal Mail* is on a boat train, climbing the sweeping curve through the closed Monkton and Came Halt to penetrate the South Dorset Downs at Bincombe tunnel. Looking south from the northern entrance to Bincombe tunnel *(below)* a rebuilt Bulleid Pacific is heading for Weymouth with a local train. Note the beautifully kept state of the embankments and track, the GWR pattern signals reflecting the joint usage of the line from Dorchester, and the siding by the signalbox to accommodate engines banking trains from Weymouth. Though any driver could ask for assistance, a banking engine for passenger trains of 10 coaches or over was usual, and anything over 12 mandatory.

Tunnel portals were always interesting locations for pictures not least Wallers Ash located in a deep straight chalk cutting. Rebuilt 'West Country' Pacific No 34095 *Brentor* is about to enter the tunnel with an up train. Once again I have been lucky enough to capture the coal washers in action on the tender to keep the dust down in the swirling air inside the bore. These washers were worked off the back injector and controlled by a small cock adjacent to the coal watering hose. The box at the rear of the tender houses the three vacuum reservoirs.

Left:
At the north end of Bincombe tunnel Standard Class 4 4-6-0 No 75076 emerges with a local train for Bournemouth. No 75076 was one of the last batch of 15 allocated to the Southern Region and was fitted with a double chimney and BR 1B tender. The west facing chalk bank behind the engine was well stocked with orchids during May.

This page:
One of the undoubted highlights of an afternoon's photography in the Weymouth area was the departure of the up Channel Islands boat train. The train first negotiated the parked boats and cars on the line from the Quay. On this occasion the train was taken over by a rebuilt Bulleid Pacific, No 34097 *Holsworthy*. The engine is loaded to 11 BR Standard and Bulleid coaches and is being banked up to Bincombe by a Standard Class 4 4-6-0. On a bright breezy summer day the train is seen *(left)* approaching Upwey & Broadwey station. In the lower picture *(below)* the station is to the left with the rolling contours of the South Dorset Downs dominating the skyline.

Left:
Since it was published in the first edition of the book, many people have asked for copies of this picture. I often took my son on photographic trips to the line and here he is on a gate near Fleet watching an up train on a misty morning in the winter of 1966/67 accompanied by his apparently amazed bear.

Below left and below:
I mentioned the long down platform at Bournemouth in an earlier caption. From it the spotters in this picture *(below left)* are enjoying an uninterrupted view of the shed. Signs of modernisation are clear with the third-rail in place and a Crompton Type 3 diesel standing by the shed. These locos were destined to spend many years on the push and pull service between Bournemouth and Weymouth. In place of the 'M7s', 'T9s' and 'King Arthurs' of earlier times, the shed yard contains BR Standard Class 4 and 5 types and a rebuilt Bulleid Pacific. In front of the shed's turntable *(below)* attention is centred on an unrebuilt Bulleid Pacific No 34023 *Blackmore Vale* which by this time has lost its nameplate. A sandbox cover on the loco has been left open allowing water to wet the sand inside rendering it useless. Together with No 34102 *Lapford*, No 34023 was the last unrebuilt Bulleid Pacific in service and happily saved from scrap by the Bulleid Society.

Left:
In the evening light rebuilt Bulleid Pacific No 34021 has paused at Parkstone station, with an up train for Weymouth. The start in the up direction from Parkstone station is on a 1 in 60 gradient which could be difficult for the driver of a heavy train.

Right:
Further down the line towards Weymouth at Upwey station, the crew of rebuilt Bulleid Pacific No 34004 pass a friendly greeting with a hurrying mother watched by my son. She is no doubt on her way to do some shopping in the seaside town and though her little boy appears to be somewhat overawed by the size of the engine, it would have been a much more exciting journey than using the bus.

Below:
Though the lighting could be difficult on the east to west aligned Woking to Basingstoke section, this stretch of line came into its own photographically towards the end of the day especially during the autumn and winter months. Late on a still October afternoon in 1964 rebuilt 'Merchant Navy' No 35002 *Union Castle* is heading westward into the sunset through Brookwood with the 4.35pm 'Royal Wessex' from Waterloo to Weymouth.

Left:
On a warm summer morning Standard Class 5 4-6-0 No 73093 is leaving the neat station of Upwey & Broadwey with a local train from Bournemouth to Weymouth. No 73093 was one of a number of Standard Class 5s allocated to the Southern Region to replace the withdrawn Maunsell classes. The white staining on the engine is probably caused by limescale out of the safety valves when the engine may have primed on some occasion often unintentionally caused by the use of water treatment briquettes at Weymouth.

Below left:
Upwey & Broadwey station again looking south towards Weymouth with a train just leaving. The Abbotsbury branch came in from the right of the picture behind the up line platform buildings, and the site of the junction can be seen at the end of the platform.

Above right:
At Hamworthy Junction a spur went off in the up direction to join the Somerset & Dorset line at Broadstone Junction. Standard Class 4 2-6-0 No 76005 is coming into the station with a local train from Bournemouth to Weymouth composed of a three-coach Bulleid set. To the left of the picture is the up starting signal controlling the junction to the Somerset & Dorset line.

Right:
Here rebuilt 'West Country' No 34047 *Callington* is leaving Dorchester South station with a train for Bournemouth. After running in from Weymouth on the up main line (second from the bottom of the picture), the train has reversed into the single platform before recommencing its journey eastward. The alignment of this platform would have been on the route of the projected 'Devon & Dorset Railway' from Exeter to Dorchester.

The next pictures show unrebuilt Bulleid Light Pacifics at work in their last years of service. No 34076 *41 Squadron* is waiting to leave Waterloo *(above left)* with the 12.54pm train to Basingstoke and Salisbury, whilst in the foreground Post Office staff assemble trolleys of mail on the adjacent platform. Mail features in this view *(below left)* of No 34038 *Lynton* running over the level crossing into Wareham station with a Waterloo to Weymouth train. No 34038 became thickly coated in oily grime towards the end despite the unofficial cleaning efforts of the spotters depicted earlier in the book. No 34015 *Exmouth* was one of the last locos in service, being withdrawn in April 1967, and is seen here *(above)* coasting non-stop through Basingstoke on a summer Saturday with a down train. To the left a through train from the London Midland Region is just leaving and in the background a 'Peak' diesel is waiting to take a train on to the north. On summer evenings the sun moved round to the north of the line on the Basingstoke-Woking stretch, and these conditions have helped to produce this striking picture *(below)* of No 34102 *Lapford* at Sturt Lane Junction on an up freight train of very mixed stock.

Above:
In 1962 unrebuilt 'Battle of Britain' Pacific No 34064 *Fighter Command* was fitted with a Giesl ejector, but because of the cost no further locos were dealt with. Unlike the other unrebuilt Pacifics this engine threw the exhaust up well which greatly assisted visibility for the driver. For the fireman, No 34064 required a different firing technique with a level fire over the grate area. Here the engine is rounding the curve by milepost 31 at Pirbright, which marked the end of the climb through Woking and Brookwood, with a train to Bournemouth.

Below:
The funeral service for Sir Winston Churchill took place in St Paul's Cathedral on 30 January 1965. Having seen the service on television my wife and I decided to go up to Waterloo to photograph the funeral train which is seen leaving at 1.28pm on its journey to Handborough hauled by No 34051 *Winston Churchill*. St Paul's Cathedral can be seen on the misty horizon. The train, which was in the charge of Nine Elms crew driver A. Hurley and fireman Jimmy Lester, consisted of five Pullman cars and bogie van No 2464.

Above:
A favourite location for generations of steam age railway photographers was Worting Junction and the adjacent Battledown flyover which took the up Bournemouth line over the tracks of the Exeter route. On a summer Saturday morning in 1964 unrebuilt Bulleid Pacific No 34065 *Hurricane* is coasting down from the flyover with an inter-regional train for the north. It has been routed on to the slow line as it will be branching off at Basingstoke for Reading West and Oxford.

Below:
Eastleigh shed's unrebuilt Bulleid Pacific No 34041 *Wilton* is pulling out of Basingstoke with a train from Oxford and the north, whilst in the down local platform sister engine No 34051 *Winston Churchill* takes water.

Left:
On 16 April 1966 blue liveried
War Department 2-10-0
No 600 *Gordon* made a very
rare sight, whilst working on
Southern Region metals
pulling out of Woking on a
non-stop run to Liss with an
RCTS railtour to the
Longmoor Military Railway.
No 600 is now based on the
Severn Valley Railway.

Below:
The line from Waterloo to
Southampton was for the most
part superbly aligned, and
especially between Basingstoke
and Woking, conducive to high
speed running. Something of
the character of this stretch of
track is shown in this winter
afternoon view of a down train
in Deepcut near Pirbright. In
the distance the LSWR lower
quadrant signals and the
hanging smoke indicate the
passage of another train.

Right:

Those who lived through the winter of 1962/3 will always remember long weeks of grey skies when the temperature rarely seemed to get above freezing. These conditions naturally put an extra strain on the Southern Region because of the vulnerability of the third-rail to snow and ice. In this picture taken at Vauxhall the winter before, a 4SUB EMU on a Windsor line train for Richmond and Twickenham approaches the station out of the gloom. To the right a stopping train from Salisbury pulls away after a signal check behind 'King Arthur' class 4-6-0 No 30796 *Sir Dodinas Le Savage.*

Below:

In total contrast, Bulleid Pacific No 34005 *Barnstaple* heads west past Berrylands station on a summer evening. No 34005 was the first light Pacific to be rebuilt being returned to traffic in June 1957. To its right a 4SUB approaches the wooden platform with an up train from Hampton Court.

Left:
Micheldever station was a remote spot in the Hampshire downland some distance north of the village it served. The station was mainly known for its extensive sidings where rolling stock destined for repair or scrap at Eastleigh works was stored. In this picture rebuilt Bulleid Pacific No 34001 *Exeter* is on the up main line of the short four track section through the station. The portal of Popham No 2 tunnel can be seen in the background. A fascinating collection of stock is stored in the sidings, notably part of a three-coach SE&CR 'Birdcage' set.

Below left:
Looking southward above Popham No 2 tunnel, a rebuilt Bulleid Pacific is leaving Micheldever station on a misty morning in 1966, past sidings full of Maunsell and Bulleid main line coaches, a present day preservationists' paradise.

Above:
An earlier picture has shown something of the tortuous line between Northam and Southampton Central. Here is 'Merchant Navy' No 35028 *Clan Line* coasting slowly out of Southampton tunnel with an up train. Smoke rolling from the chimney fills the confines of the cutting, and safety valves have lifted as a result of the good fire built up for the long climb through Winchester to the summit at Litchfield tunnel.

Left:
In the last days of steam the Bournemouth line saw a number of visiting engines, such as the already preserved Gresley 'A4' Pacific No 4498 *Sir Nigel Gresley*. On 3 June 1967, with little over a month to go before the start of full electrification, the loco worked a railtour from Waterloo to Bournemouth. In this picture the train is leaving Bournemouth Central.

Above:
An interesting regular working on weekdays was the up afternoon stock train from Eastleigh to Clapham Junction loop which often contained ex-works coaches in its formation. In this 1960 picture taken near Winchfield, the train was hauled by the usual Maunsell 'H15' class 4-6-0 No 30476 which has an ex-works Bulleid brake coach behind the tender followed by a Maunsell open 3rd.

Below:
Through trains from the Western Region added variety and interest to workings west of Basingstoke. Here 'Hall' class 4-6-0 No 6970 *Whaddon Hall* is climbing away from Brockenhurst with a train from the Midlands composed of BR Standard stock. Lymington Junction signalbox can be seen above the first coach, and to the right of the picture, the Lymington branch.

Above right:
Bournemouth West station was comparatively little photographed compared to its large neighbour some three miles up the line but was particularly interesting because it was the starting point for Somerset & Dorset Line trains. Others went to Salisbury such as 'T9' 4-4-0 No 30313 awaiting departure in 1958 for the 38-mile journey to the cathedral city and its home shed. One of the Bulleid early main line corridor sets makes up the train.

Below right:
A train I always tried to photograph on the main line was the early Saturday afternoon goods from Woking to Basingstoke which was rostered for a Feltham Maunsell 'S15' 4-6-0, here No 30840. On this damp afternoon the locomotive is working hard on the climb through Brookwood station, its task not made easier by the dead weight of an 0-6-0 diesel shunter behind the tender. The diesel is probably en route to Eastleigh works.

Above left:
Because of the three-mile severe climb from 'cold' out of Weymouth to Bincombe tunnel at a ruling gradient of 1 in 50, double-heading was common on this stretch. Radipole Halt was opened by the GWR to serve the northern outskirts of Weymouth though few trains stopped there in latter years and it closed in 1984. In this picture the Halt has retained its characteristic 'Pagoda' waiting shelters and gas lamps. On a winter morning Standard Class 5 4-6-0 No 73169 is piloting a Standard Class 4 4-6-0 through the Halt on an up special train. The effects of the exhaust from the two engines is not going to improve the whiteness of the washing hanging high on a line in the garden of one of the houses overlooking the station, some of which were lived in by local railwaymen.

Below left:
Among the most memorable special trains to run out of Waterloo in the last years of steam were the two tours that ran on 2 and 16 December 1962 as a farewell to the Beattie '0298' class 2-4-0WTs. These trains (the second being a repeat tour) ran from Waterloo to Hampton Court, Chessington and Shepperton in beautifully crisp cold weather. The overnight frost is still on the sleepers as Nos 30585 and 30587 come past Wimbledon West yard on the down slow line en route to Hampton Court on 2 December.

Above:
I suppose the chances of capturing consecutively numbered engines passing on the road were very slight but here are Nos 73111 *King Uther* (though it has lost its nameplate) on an up local train passing sister engine No 73112 *Morgan Le Fay* on a down boat train to Southampton New Docks. This batch of Standard Class 5 4-6-0s were named after the 'King Arthur' class and the design of the lettering of the nameplates was based on the originals.

Below:
Once again I was lucky at Battledown flyover to capture two trains: on the left rebuilt Bulleid Pacific No 34021 *Dartmoor* on a train to Exeter, and on the right Feltham's 'S15' class 4-6-0 No 30840 is on a freight for Southampton Docks.

I derived a great deal of pleasure from panning some of my shots and here are four of the best examples. I have used my Voightlander Bessa II camera, which gave eight 6cm x 9cm negatives on a film, for all these pictures. I had two Bessa IIs, the first with a Color-Skopar lens and the second with a five element Color-Heliar, both with Synchro-Compur shutters. Generally speaking I found that 1/100th second was best for panning and the Voightlander 'Kontur' viewfinder I used on the top of the camera was a tremendous aid to success since it gave a bright clear image and could be used keeping both eyes open which was a great help. The picture of No 34009 *Lyme Regis (above)* was taken as the loco sped down the bank from Bincombe tunnel to

Weymouth and shows much detail on the top of the engine not normally visible. On a duller day *(centre left)* No 34023 *Blackmore Vale*, with driver Harry Pope from Nine Elms on the footplate, is forging west near Weybridge with a down Bournemouth train. The Windsor line platforms at Clapham Junction were a good location in the evening for panning work, and rails in the sidings have accentuated the sense of speed *(bottom left)* as No 34018 *Axminster* leans to the curve with a down train. In this illusion in speed *(below)* No 73118 on an up train at Clapham Junction appears to have been overtaken by the BAC 1-11 on the hoarding advertising British United Airways!

Above:
With completion of the first stage of the Kent Coast electrification in June 1959, a number of surplus locomotives were transferred from the Eastern to Western section. Among these were 4-4-0s of Classes D1, E1 and L1. In this picture taken at Nine Elms in 1959, 'L1s' Nos 31786 and 31787 (known by engineman as 'glasshouses' because of the glazed side window in the cab) are standing out of use, with 'D1' No 31505 to their left in store with its chimney covered. With adequate numbers of Standard classes and Bulleid Pacifics there was very little work for these 4-4-0s at Nine Elms, though the 'D1s' did appear on parcels trains, and an 'L1' was regularly rostered for the 12.42pm (SO) train from Waterloo to Basingstoke. This picture contrasts the design of the 'D1' and 'L1' tenders, and the almost dainty proportions of the former.

Right:
'T9' No 30117 was another of the venerable 4-4-0s working on the Southern in the late 1950s. After the onset of the Hampshire dieselisation scheme a few 'T9s' remained at Eastleigh in the late 1950s and were employed on a variety of turns such as the seasonal strawberry specials originating in the Swanwick and Fareham districts. However, no such work is on offer for No 30117 on this misty winter day at Eastleigh where I photographed the engine framed in the shed doorway.

Right:
Some pleasing evening views of Basingstoke shed and the adjacent main line could be obtained from the path which led to the back of the building. By the time this picture was taken in 1965 Standard types had long since ousted the 'Remembrance' class with which the shed was particularly associated. Three Standard classes are on view, 2-6-4T No 80065, 2-6-0 No 76067 and a Class 4 4-6-0 in the 75000 series. In the background a rebuilt Bulleid Pacific is leaving on a down train.

Below:
The turntable at Nine Elms shed was probably out of use, and the two 'Merchant Navy' Pacifics and 'Schools' 4-4-0 in this picture have used the triangle in the loco yard and are waiting to reverse under the coaling tower before moving into the main shed yard. Starting an engine up the slope towards the main line on a wet day could be difficult because of the accumulated grease and oil on the rails. Loco Shed Junction signalbox and Battersea power station can be glimpsed in the left background.

Left:
The interior of Eastleigh shed in 1958 where one of its distinguished elderly residents, 'T9' 4-4-0 No 30120, has been enjoying the attention of the cleaners who have now moved on to the Standard Class 4 behind. The scene is lit by sunlight shafting down from the roof through air heavy with the smell of paraffin and smoke.

Below left:
On 26 March 1966 Gresley 'A4' Pacific No 60024 *Kingfisher* worked a special train for the 'A4' Preservation Society from Waterloo to Weymouth returning via Yeovil Pen Mill and Junction. Here during a break in the journey at Eastleigh the engine is standing outside the main line end of the shed for photography by the tour participants.

Above:
Because of its proximity to the Works, Eastleigh shed was invariably fascinating to visit, the occasion on which this picture was taken being no exception. I suspect the majority of locos in this line-up are destined for the works or scrap. They are classes 'E6' 0-6-2T, two '0298' 2-4-0WTs from Wadebridge, 'Q' 0-6-0, 'S15' 4-6-0, 'A1X' 0-6-0T, 'B4' 0-4-0T, '02' 0-4-4T, 'T9' 4-4-0, 'M7' 0-4-4T and 'U' class 2-6-0.

Left:
Light, shade and steam in sheds could produce some lovely effects which sadly cannot be faithfully captured in preservation. Here a rebuilt 'Battle of Britain' Pacific catches the light just inside Nine Elms depot as its boiler is blown down. The loco's nameplate has been removed for safe keeping, exposing the ugly backing plate.

65

Left:
Two pictures taken at Bournemouth using my Bronica camera, the first *(top)* of rebuilt Bulleid Pacific No 34093 deep in the shed surrounded by leaking steam. The exposure was always tricky for these shots, and a fast film like HP3 was essential since I never used flash which would have spoilt the natural lighting effects. Meanwhile outside the shed offices *(bottom)* a driver reads the notice board by the mess rooms before going on duty. To the right is one of the Brush diesels that were used to supplement steam on Bournemouth line expresses during the lead up to electrification. The angle of the light in this picture has picked out the solid coating of dirt and grease on the brick walkways between the rails, so typical of steam sheds.

Right:
I was always keen to include railway staff in my pictures — here is driver Peter Miller of Weymouth shed seemingly dwarfed by a Standard Class 5 4-6-0 which he is preparing before leaving the shed to take a train for Bournemouth.

Below right:
At Bournemouth shed the fireman of rebuilt Bulleid Pacific No 35023 is silhouetted against the engine on a summer evening.

Left:
The fireman of this Bulleid
Pacific at Bournemouth shed
seems to have forgotten that
his engine's tender is more
than full, and whilst very bad
working practice, has provided
a dramatic picture. The high
shutter speed used on my
Bronica camera (1/500th sec)
has captured the pattern of the
overflowing water.

Right:
Nearly all trains stopping at
Southampton Central would
take water, and some smart
work was required to avoid
delay, especially if the train
was running late. The tender
of this LMS Class 5 is full and
the driver is pulling the chain
to re-position the water hose
over the drain on the platform
ramp.

Below right:
The Bronica camera came into
its own in sheds where many
detailed pictures could be
taken requiring precise
focusing and composition.
This study at Bournemouth
shed is centred round a water
column chain.

Above:
Coal dust was a constant
nuisance for footplate staff
especially when the coal was of
poor quality. Here the fireman
of a Standard Class 5 4-6-0 is
playing his pep pipe on to the
piled up coal in the tender
before leaving Bournemouth
Central for Waterloo.

Left:
Another detail study of a loco's
brake and steam pipes at
Bournemouth shed. Water
drips steadily into the flooded
space between the rails.

This page:
Two pictures of driver Peter Miller at Weymouth shed, the first (above) showing him oiling the horn cheek boxes of rebuilt Bulleid Pacific No 35014 Nederland Line. To fully prepare a rebuilt Pacific for the road took about 50 minutes, though the unrebuilt version could be prepared in about half this time, since for example it had only six corks on each side of the engine. In the second picture (left) Weymouth shed fireman John Bonney has checked the sand, fire and water of rebuilt 'Battle of Britain' class No 34087 145 Squadron and is climbing down from the cab watched by Peter. The engine will be shortly leaving the shed to take over the afternoon Channel Islands boat train to Waterloo. The yellow triangle below the number indicates that the engine is fitted with BR boiler water treatment.

This set of four pictures shows something of the dirty and hard work that was involved in servicing a locomotive for its next turn of duty. Rebuilt Bulleid Pacific No 35028 *Clan Line* has come on shed at Weymouth and the shedman is clearing the smokebox of char using a large No 8 size shovel *(left)* and emptying the ashpan of clinker *(right)*. Shed staff found that smokebox char was very good for keeping slugs at bay on their allotments! Later *(below)* the engine is carefully positioned and balanced on the turntable and all 151 tons pushed round by the fireman. The all important correct balancing of the engine could be sensed through the upright lever before it was pushed down allowing the turntable to be rotated.

Left:
A powerful picture of double chimney Standard Class 4 No 75076 waiting its next turn of duty at Weymouth shed. These useful engines worked goods and secondary passenger services from Weymouth and in general took over the duties undertaken by the Maunsell 'King Arthur' and 'H15' classes, all withdrawn by the early 1960s.

Above:
A Standard Class 4 2-6-4T almost dwarfed by piles of ash awaiting removal at Bournemouth shed, a reflection of the difficulty in recruiting staff towards the end of steam to undertake this dirty and onerous work.

Right:
I have used a slow shutter speed on the Bronica camera to give a sense of movement to the steam and water escaping from these injector pipes on a locomotive at Bournemouth shed.

The interior of the spacious shed at Nine Elms was full of atmosphere as I think these three pictures show. On a Sunday morning *(left)* a rebuilt Bulleid Pacific is slumbering at the end of one of the shed roads with smoke from a recently lit fire rolling out of its chimney. Further over *(below)* two more Pacifics, No 35021 *New Zealand Line* and No 35026 *Lamport & Holt Line,* await further duties. When these pictures were taken steam still had a few years to go and the locomotives have the appearance of being well cared for, as Nine Elms could still recruit cleaners. Further down the shed *(right)* towards the entrance, 'Battle of Britain' Pacific No 34077 *603 Squadron* presents a dramatic and powerful profile against the sunlight shafting from the roof through the smoke.

Some of the most interesting detail pictures of locomotives were of their wheels. Rebuilt Bulleid Pacific No 34052 *Lord Dowding (above left)* has been into Eastleigh works for attention and I could not resist posing my then diminutive son in front of the solid 6ft 2in diameter bulk of the Bulleid-Firth-Brown centre driving wheel. *(above right)*. The driving wheel and motion of the now preserved 'King Arthur' No 30777 Sir *Lamiel* is rather more elegant in design, but shows evidence of some 35 years of hard honest toil. In this picture *(right)* of rebuilt Bulleid Pacific No 34039 *Boscastle* at Eastleigh shed, the angled light has thrown into relief the gleaming sides of the loco and its oily motion. The blur produced by wheels and motion at speed was not easy to capture, but in this picture *(left)* taken one sunny evening near Winchester Junction, I have stood near the track and panned the camera using 1/500th second.

Left:
The grass grown sidings at the back of Eastleigh shed bordering on what was then a quiet airfield, were the haunt of withdrawn engines. On a dismal wet day in March 1961 '0415' class 4-4-2T No 30584, finally displaced from service on the Lyme Regis branch, and 'T9' 4-4-0 No 30288, once a contender for preservation, await cutting up.

Below:
A happier scene finds 'T9' No 30709 from Exmouth Junction shed undergoing what would have been a last general overhaul at Eastleigh works in 1958. No 30709 was among the last handful of active 'T9s' based in the West Country, and spent much of its time sub shedded at Okehampton.

Right:
Outside the works Exmouth Junction's gleaming unrebuilt 'Merchant Navy' Pacific No 35001 *Channel Packet* has completed a general overhaul and is ready for transfer to the running shed and return to the West Country.

Below :
Looking very different from its unrebuilt sister, rebuilt No 35022 *Holland America Line* is nearly ready for traffic. Through the kindness of the Southern Region, visits to the works could be arranged on weekdays, which gave the opportunity to picture not only the locomotives, but also the staff who were overhauling them.

Above:
Unlike today when we all seem to want sun to light our pictures, I was happy to photograph in all conditions. Driving towards Micheldever station one wet and stormy evening I saw a break developing in the clouds sweeping over the downland. After running across the fields, I was able to capture this dramatic view of a Standard Class 4 pulling away from Wallers Ash loop with an up cement train.

Below:
At Steventon between Worting Junction and Micheldever, the line ran along a high embankment, which allowed me to take this picture of a rebuilt Bulleid Pacific on a down train silhouetted against the evening sky.

Below right:
Coronet for steam — this silhouette of No 34001 *Exeter* photographed against shafts of light, was taken one still summer evening near Radipole Halt.

There are few photographers who have not used trees at some time to frame their pictures and give them depth, and I often did so. I have used the branches of an oak to add interest to this picture *(above)* taken near Winchfield on an early Spring afternoon of a down Bournemouth train; *(left)* large trees growing by the lineside away from cuttings or embankments were not that common, but this one north of Winchester Junction sets off perfectly a Standard Class 5 working a train of empty coal wagons. West of Wool station the Bournemouth to Weymouth line ran across the desolate pine clad Winfrith Heath. Here *(above right)* the passengers in this up train hauled by a Standard Class 4 2-6-0, are snug in their Bulleid coaches as a raw wind sweeps across from the south-west. Near Lymington Junction the main line ran across heather covered heathland with few trees *(right)*, but a single windswept pine frames an Ivatt 2-6-2T No 41320 working an enthusiasts' special in the last days of steam.

Top:
A Standard Class 4 76000 series 2-6-0 leaves Dorchester South with a stopping train for Bournemouth Central. The overbridge from which this picture was taken gives a good view of the track layout in the immediate vicinity of the station and the new signalbox brought into use in February 1959.

Above:
Another Class 4 2-6-0 No 76010 runs into Weymouth station with a local train from Bournemouth composed of Bulleid stock. This picture shows something of the extensive platforms and sidings, and behind the van at the rear of the train, the modern signalbox.

Right:
On a bright autumn afternoon near Millbrook, a 'U' class Mogul No 31626 makes a pleasing sight heading for Salisbury with a neat train of Bulleid stock. The fireman has been careless in leaving the front coupling on the engine hanging free when it should have been hooked up against the buffer beam.

Below:
Summer Saturdays on the main line could sometimes produce surprises such as this ex-LBSCR 'K' class Mogul No 32339 well away from its usual duties on the Central Section, hurrying along near Hook with a Basingstoke to Waterloo stopping train. In earlier years other LBSCR classes had been seen on the line, for example 'B4X' 4-4-0s extracted from store, on Farnborough Air Show trains in the early 1950s.

Left:
It is a warm summer evening and after a day's work, members of the Phoenix Tennis Club at New Malden are enjoying a game, probably unaware of Feltham's 'S15' class No 30834 thumping past in a pall of sulphurous smoke with the 7.02pm vans train from Waterloo.

Below:
Down at Brockenhurst 'M7' No 30328 is propelling a Lymington train out of Brockenhurst. In this 1959 picture the train consists of a Urie 'Ironclad' two-coach push and pull set. No 30328 was one of the handful of 'M7s' later transferred for work on the Central Section, notably push and pull workings from Tunbridge Wells West and Three Bridges, though they did not prove popular with the Brighton line enginemen.

Above:
A wide variety of locomotive types could be seen at Basingstoke on summer Saturday trains in the 1950s and early 1960s. In 1965 a '9F' No 92001 is leaving the station with a through train for the Midlands, and in the siding to the left a Western Region 'Hall' 4-6-0 is waiting its turn of duty.

Below:
Displaced by the Kent Coast electrification 'L' class 4-4-0 No 31768 was transferred to Nine Elms in 1959 in the hope of finding gainful employment. Like the 'L1' and 'D1' 4-4-0s shown earlier, No 31768 spent most of its time out of use, but December 1960 sees it working a Christmas parcels train through Vauxhall.

Right:
Class 5 4-6-0s were regularly seen south of Basingstoke, for example No 44942 passing the closed Shawford Junction in the summer of 1966 with what is probably the 10.08am York to Poole train, due at Southampton about 5.30pm.

Below:
Rebuilt Bulleid Pacific No 34028 *Eddystone* was the first of the class to be withdrawn in May 1964. Flanked by Feltham Urie 'S15' No 30510 waiting to run down to the Southampton Docks for a freight, No 34028 is coming north past Bevois Park yard just south of St Denys station with a train for Waterloo. No 34028 still survives currently being restored to working order on a farm at Lyminge, Kent.

Above:
Durnsford Road power station was constructed by the LSWR to provide current for its suburban electrification, and was demolished in 1964. Rebuilt 'Battle of Britain' No 34050 *Royal Observer Corps* is passing with a summer Saturday train for Bournemouth. Under the cabside number can be seen the 'Long Service' ROC medal ribbon which the engine was awarded in July 1961 to mark 12 years in operation.

Right:
Here is the 5.43pm train to Salisbury again, hauled by rebuilt 'West Country' No 34013 *Okehampton* passing the flyover at Wimbledon which takes the up slow over the two fast lines. No 34013 was a regular engine on this train. This service was worked by Nine Elms enginemen and fireman Mick Roberts is looking back at me from the cab of No 34013. In the distance a 2BIL electric unit is on an up semi-fast from Alton.

Southampton — at the Terminus station in 1958 *(above)* 'T9' No 30707 shunts its train for Bournemouth West whilst a Churchward '4300' class 2-6-0 has arrived earlier with a train from Andover. In the background is the liner *Queen Mary*. At the Central station *(below)* rebuilt 'West Country' Pacific No 34017 *Ilfracombe* has lost its feet on the greasy rails with what may be the 4.20pm SO train for Waterloo. On the approach to Southampton *(above right)* No 35005 *Canadian Pacific* brings a Waterloo train round the curve near Millbrook. Some of the roads near the Central station *(below right)* offered the opportunity to picture the trains against the background of the New Docks such as No 35008 *Orient Line* leaving for Bournemouth. Behind the train is the liner *Australis* then owned by the Chandris Line. The *Australis* was built in 1940 in Newport, Virginia as the *America*, at 33,000 tons then the largest ship built in the USA. She was bought by the Chandris Line in 1964 to be used largely on voyages for immigrants from the UK and Greece to Australia and New Zealand.

This page:
Level crossings were always interesting places for pictures especially where they incorporated a footbridge as here *(right)* at Mount Pleasant Crossing near Northam. On a hot summer afternoon, rebuilt Pacific No 34005 *Barnstaple* is heading towards Eastleigh. whilst pedestrians and the drivers of a Morris 1000 car and a motor cycle wait patiently to cross the tracks. Further down the line at Poole *(below)*, traffic in steam days was frequently interrupted by trains to Weymouth and the Somerset & Dorset. This freight for Weymouth in the charge of Standard Class 4 2-6-0 No 76026 is slowly coasting round the curves towards the station. Note the wide pedestrian gates on the far side of the level crossing presumably to accommodate the passage of bicycles.

Opposite:
It must be market day at Dorchester *(right)* judging by the mothers waiting for rebuilt 'Merchant Navy' No 35023 to come to a stand at Upwey & Broadwey in 1966 with a substantial train for Bournemouth. The passengers will enjoy their short journey in main line comfort with plenty of space for their prams. No 35023 had by this time lost its nameplate and was almost at the end of a distinguished career which included top link trains on the Waterloo-Exeter line. Only spotters can be seen on the up platform at Basingstoke *(below right)* in the pouring rain. John Roscoe, the fireman of rebuilt 'West Country' No 34026 *Yes Tor*, wearing the standard Nine Elms fireman's headgear of a knotted handkerchief, is looking out for the 'right away' signal. Behind, a 'Hall' class 4-6-0 is backing down on to a train for the Western Region.

Left:
Apart from filling in time working secondary services to Basingstoke and Salisbury, the 'Schools' 4-4-0s displaced from Kent performed some excellent work on the heavy Lymington boat trains. I photographed No 30902 *Wellington* on an up working accelerating away from a signal check near Beaulieu Road, and would have been able to enjoy the loco's deep rhythmic three-cylinder beat and the characteristic ring of the coupling rods.

Below:
At St Denys unrebuilt 'West Country' No 34008 *Padstow* has just joined the main line with the through train from Brighton to Bournemouth. The three disc route code the locomotive is displaying gave an air of the unusual to the train since most codes were only two disc. In the foreground is a reminder of the plots of lineside land that were cultivated by railwaymen, and this gardener looks likely to enjoy a good crop of rhubarb and cabbages.

Above:
The afternoon boat train to Waterloo is pulling away up the
1 in 187 gradient out of Weymouth behind rebuilt 'Battle of
Britain' Pacific No 34082 *615 Squadron*. The train is fairly lightly
loaded with only six coaches and a van, but is being banked by a
Standard Class 4 2-6-0 which will come off at Bincombe. The
shed can be seen behind the front coach of the train.

Below:
Over on the Windsor line side at Clapham Junction rebuilt 'West
Country' Pacific No 34021 *Dartmoor* is running into Platform 3
with an up empty stock train which has travelled via East
Putney. To the right unusually clean 'Q1' No 33020 is on station
pilot duties. No 33020 was destined to be one of the last three
'Q1s' in service being withdrawn from Guildford shed in January
1966.

This page:
'Lord Nelson' No 30856 *Lord St Vincent*, one of the last 'Lord Nelsons' in service, was withdrawn from Eastleigh in September 1962. Here are two pictures of the loco in its final year or so of service *(above)* working the heavy 5.09pm commuter train to Basingstoke through Vauxhall, and *(below)* on an evening train to Bournemouth composed of eleven smartly turned out Bulleid coaches, passing Raynes Park.

Opposite:
Two other classes which became extinct in the early 1960s were the Eastleigh series of 'King Arthurs' and the Drummond '700' class 0-6-0s. 'Eastleigh Arthur' No 30451 *Sir Lamorak (above right)* is seen leaving Oatlands cutting near Weybridge with an up Christmas parcels train one December morning in 1961. The engine was cut up in July 1962. The competent Drummond '700' class 0-6-0s were long associated with the London area, though somewhat overshadowed by their more charismatic sisters, the 'T9' class. Here *(below right)* No 30694 is crossing from the up main line at Wimbledon to gain access to the West Yard with the evening pick-up goods from Surbiton in 1959.

Left:
**Rebuilt Bulleid 'West Country'
Pacific No 34044 *Woolacombe*
is in the clean cut incision
through the chalk on the
approach to the north end of
Wallers Ash tunnel, clearly
showing the superb alignment
of the London & Southampton
Railway and the remote open
downland it passes through.
Today this is one of the few
remaining areas of truly open
country between London and
the Hampshire coast.**

Below:
**Further west a rebuilt 'West
Country' is crossing through
the South Dorset Downs and
beginning the descent down
the ruling gradient of 1 in 91
towards Dorchester.**

Above:
This picture shows something of the bleakness of Winfrith Heath between Wool and Moreton with little shelter apart from a few pine trees. A Standard Class 5 on a train for Weymouth is about to cross an up train hauled by a Standard Class 4 2-6-0.

Below:
The lovely clear afternoon of Easter Monday 1966 sees a Standard Class 4 4-6-0 and Standard Class 5 4-6-0 toiling up the 1 in 50 bank out of Weymouth towards Bincombe tunnel with a 12-coach train of Bulleid stock. The clump of trees to the right of the line was known as 'two-mile copse' by the local enginemen. The effect of a strong cross wind on a passenger train on this exposed embankment could reduce the speed by 10-15mph. This hillside position by the closed Upwey Wishing Well Halt was a favourite with photographers, giving a superb view of the line, as well as a panorama over Weymouth and the Isle of Portland, which can be seen on the right of the picture.

The inclusion of water always adds to a picture and here are four examples where this was possible on the Winchester to Weymouth section. East Stoke level crossing was a delightful spot between Wareham and Wool, *(left)* where the River Frome ran alongside the railway for a short stretch. I have photographed rebuilt 'West Country' No 34021 coming up from Weymouth with the afternoon Channel Islands boat train. Rain is threatening, but a brighter patch to the west has lit the scene nicely. The aptly name River Piddle or Trent is running fairly high *(below)* through the water meadows outside Wareham one winter afternoon in 1963 as a rebuilt 'West Country' Pacific pulls away from the station with a Weymouth train. Further up the line between Eastleigh and Shawford *(right)*, 'West Country' Pacific No 34004 *Yeovil* heads north alongside the River Itchen swollen by winter rain. Whilst not a natural feature, the large boating lake at Poole provided an interesting setting. On a windy day *(below right)* a rebuilt Bulleid Pacific is beginning the 1 in 60 climb to Parkstone with an up train.

Above:
Between Weybridge and Byfleet the main line crossed the Wey Navigation. From its towpath I have photographed rebuilt 'West Country' No 34101 *Hartland* on a down train. Timing for this sort of picture was difficult since, whilst the train could be heard approaching, it was only briefly in shot.

Left:
One golden evening in late summer when the sun had moved round to light up the north side of the line, I photographed a rebuilt 'West Country' Pacific by the River Mole near Esher with a down train.

Above right:
Crossing the small viaduct spanning watercress beds and the River Loddon at Old Basing, rebuilt 'West Country' No 34042 *Dorchester* working a down train, has shut off steam for a stop at Basingstoke.

Right:
Against the background of a cold wintry sky, a Standard Class 5 4-6-0 pulls away from Poole and past the boating lake, its exhaust blown inland by the stiff wind off the sea.

Left:
On a cold early spring day at Beaulieu Road a strong north-west wind is bringing frequent heavy showers sweeping across the heathland which surrounds the station. Torrential rain has just cleared as a Standard 2-6-4T prepares to depart with a stopping train to Eastleigh.

Below left:
The spring weather is more seasonal in this picture of a '76000' series 2-6-0 and Standard Class 5 4-6-0 passing blossom near Radipole Halt on the climb to Bincombe tunnel. In the background rooks are nesting in the elm trees by the skew bridge carrying the main A354 road to Dorchester.

Right:
On a hot summer afternoon at East Stoke, cows enjoy the soft cool mud by the River Frome as rebuilt 'West Country' Pacific No 34021 passes on a Weymouth train.

Below:
Winter in the New Forest and ponies remain largely indifferent to the passing of a Standard Class 4 2-6-4T on a train to Lymington Pier. The 2-6-4Ts took over work from the 'M7s' on the branch. Among the 'M7s' replaced was No 30053 now repatriated from the United States and undergoing restoration for eventual use on the Swanage Railway.

Left:
Because of the influence of the sea, weather conditions were often very different a mile or two inland from Weymouth. In this picture of Standard Class 5 No 73114 and rebuilt 'Battle of Britain' No 34082 *615 Squadron* leaving Upwey & Broadwey station, sea mist was swirling in from the coast, but where I stood it was clear blue sky. A few passengers have alighted from the train and are beginning the walk down the long station drive to the road leading to the village.

Above:
On a cold clear morning unrebuilt Bulleid Pacific No 34023 *Blackmore Vale* speeds down the gradient south of Micheldever. The engine is under light steam and the drifting exhaust will be making visibility very difficult for the driver as he approaches Wallers Ash and Winchester.

Below:
On a day of sunshine and showers, Standard Class 4 4-6-0 No 75077 heads for Bincombe past the site of the closed Monkton & Came Halt. The turbulent sky behind threatens more heavy rain.

Right:
This winter day had not been very promising photographically with much slow moving cloud. However, just as the down 'Bournemouth Belle' was due through Brockenhurst, the low sun broke through the clouds, its slanting rays lighting up the exhaust of a rebuilt 'Merchant Navy' as it pounded through the station and up the bank towards Lymington Junction.

Below:
At the small level crossing at East Stoke I used my Bronica camera for this picture of a down local train receding west towards Wool.

Right:
To mark the end of what had become so familiar, the Southern Region ran two 'Farewell to Steam' specials from Waterloo to Bournemouth and to Weymouth on 2 July 1967. No 35008 *Orient Line* and No 35028 *Clan Line* were used, both specially cleaned with their nameplates restored for the occasion. Here is No 35028 climbing past Wallers Ash with the return working, the total absence of heads out of the windows being quite remarkable.

Below:
'Into the hills and far away' — perhaps this picture symbolizes the end of working steam in southern England. As a storm clears to the east a Standard Class 4 locomotive heads past sodden fields towards the lonely South Dorset Downs and Bincombe tunnel with a local train from Bournemouth.